C000186947

CANADIAN
ROCKIES

AMAZING PHOTOS™

CANADIAN ROCKIES

Darwin Wiggett

ALTITUDE PUBLISHING

Published by Altitude Publishing Canada Ltd.
1500 Railway Avenue, Canmore, Alberta T1W 1P6
www.altitudepublishing.com
1-800-957-6888

Extreme care has been taken to ensure that all information presented
in this book is accurate and up to date. Neither the photographer nor
the publisher can be held responsible for any errors.

Publisher Stephen Hutchings
Associate Publisher Kara Turner
Design and Photo Editing Stephen Hutchings
Editor Diana Marshall
Layout Bryan Pezzi

We acknowledge the financial support of the Government of Canada
through the Book Publishing Industry Development Program (BPIDP)
for our publishing activities.

 Altitude GreenTree Program: Altitude Publishing will plant twice
as many trees as were used in the manufacturing of this product.

Library and Archives Canada Cataloguing in Publication

Wiggett, Darwin, 1961-
    The Canadian Rockies / Darwin Wiggett.

(Amazing photos)
ISBN 1-55439-607-7

    1. Rocky Mountains, Canadian (B.C. and Alta.)--Pictorial works.
I. Title. II. Series.

FC219.W564 2006   971.1'050222   C2006-903172-X

An application for the trademark for Amazing Photos™ has been made
and the registered trademark is pending.

Printed and bound in Canada by Friesens
2 4 6 8 9 7 5 3 1

INTRODUCTION

To describe the breathtaking landscapes of the Canadian Rocky Mountains is an impossible task. Mere words do not adequately prepare a person for the assault on the senses that comes with first-hand experiences of the grandeur of the Rockies. Even photographs, proverbially worth a thousand words, are ill-equipped to represent the reality and intensity of the Rockies to the uninitiated.

Knowing these limitations, photographer Darwin Wiggett has attempted in this collection to present images that offer a glimpse, however small, of the magnificence of this raw and rugged wilderness — in all of its mutability. These photos resonate with the moods, the drama, the excitement, the colours, the textures, and the serenity of the Canadian Rockies.

The hope is that they will inspire you to experience this great wilderness in person. Dig deeper, wander farther, observe more closely, and begin your own journey of discovery into this sky-bound wilderness of exceptional landscapes and quiet moments.

pages 6–7:
Nothing is more rewarding than an alpine hike on a sunny
summer's day in Mount Assiniboine Provincial Park, BC.
The view across Sunburst Valley includes the majestic
Wedgewood Peak and Mount Assiniboine.

above:
Johnston Canyon, in Banff National Park, offers visitors
stunning views along a suspended catwalk: gnarled trees,
plunging cliffs, natural tunnels, and swirling mountain water
in deep chasms.

opposite:
It is easy to see why Moraine Lake, in Banff National Park, is
an iconic destination for tourists and photographers alike.
The Wenkchemna Peaks soar high above an emerald basin
of water, inspiring awe with every viewing.

above:
Bighorn sheep are a common sight for hikers trekking up to Wilcox Pass above the Columbia Icefield in Jasper National Park. A full-curl ram stands calmly in the waning alpine light.

opposite:
A nameless waterfall cascades haphazardly below Barrier Lake in Kananaskis Country.

page 14:
The lush spring foliage and luminous Alberta sky reward hikers at Mount Birdwood in Kananaskis Country.

page 15:
Every summer the meadows at Bow Summit are saturated with the magenta of fireweed, providing a perfect foreground in this photograph of Mount Crowfoot lit by the morning sun.

above:
Panther Falls are one of the highest and most impressive falls in Banff National Park, but few visitors experience the power of the water along this stretch of Nigel Creek because the falls are not marked from the Icefields Parkway.

opposite:
Chephren Lake, a picturesque day hike destination, is well worth the effort for its view of Mount Chephren.

opposite:
On sunny afternoons, rainbows dance playfully along the foot of one of the highest falls in North America — Takakkaw Falls — in Yoho National Park.

above:
Morning fog rises off Mistaya River obscuring Mount Chephren in the distance, Banff National Park.

left:
Calypso orchids bloom in May in the Canadian Rockies. Its yellow throat is normally adorned in pink petals, but this is a rare albino specimen photographed in Kananaskis Country.

above:
On cool mornings, the lakes and streams of the Canadian
Rockies are frequently shrouded in mist. On this morning,
Maligne Lake is cloaked in the blue hues of a lifting
dawn fog.

opposite:
Lake Louise, one of Canada's most sought-after destinations,
looks its most memorable at sunrise when warm light bathes
Mount Victoria in oranges and pinks.

above:
Moose are a common sight along Highway 40 in Kananaskis Country. This imposing bull was photographed in a marshy area in the fall.

opposite:
A thick stand of aspen trees creates a jumble of black and white in a meadow of yellow grass in Kananaskis Country.

30:

...ter ushers in magical transformations throughout the
kies — snow-frosted meadows and obliquely lit peaks
und. Here, Second Vermilion Lake, warmed by thermal
ngs, mirrors a glowing Mount Rundle.

31:

...te August and early September, the vegetation in Wilcox
, above the Columbia Icefield, turns a riot of colour.
four-kilometre (2.5 miles) trek to the top of the pass
...wcases the best fall colours the Rockies have to offer.

pages 32–33:
This kaleidoscope of colours around Bow Lake at Bow Summit, in Banff National Park, is just one of the reasons why September is one of the best times of the year to visit the Canadian Rockies.

above:
Hikers head to the Lake O'Hara area in Yoho National Park in large numbers. In September, the alpine larch glow an intense yellow, as seen here, along the Opabin Plateau.

opposite:
The last rays of the setting sun illuminate the distant Opal Range across Spillway Lake in Peter Lougheed Provincial Park.

unt Edith Cavell's Angel Glacier sloughs off small icebergs
ughout summer, offering visitors a sampling of winter in
heat of August.

e:
Prince of Wales Hotel, perched above Waterton Lake,
e of the most photographed hotels in North America.
views from the hotel and surrounding areas are
-inspiring.

above:
Black bears are often seen along roads in the Canadian Rockies in May and June. This beautiful creature was feasting on dandelions in Kootenay National Park when photographed.

opposite:
Spectacular views of Mount Huber, Lake O'Hara, and Mary Lake reward intrepid hikers willing to tackle the All Soul's Prospect alpine route in Yoho National Park.

above:
Ice crystals in high clouds backlit by the sun form shimmering rainbows. Common but rarely noticed, this phenomenon can be spotted with the help of polarized sunglasses.

opposite:
In early spring, before the snow melts, mountain peaks are still white and alpine rivers are low. This springtime image of Mount Fryatt and the Athabasca River, in Jasper National Park, hint at the seasonal transformations still to come.

posite:
...ount Kidd, with its jagged upper profile and grassy lower ...opes, is a familiar landmark of Peter Lougheed Provincial ...rk, Kananaskis Country.

...ove:
...ater-sculpted rocks in sinuous shapes are evidence of the ...wer of the Kicking Horse River in Yoho National Park.

...ge 48:
...cked boats at the Lake O' Hara Lodge add a human ...unterpoint to the grand vistas in Yoho National Park.

...e 49:
...lden light tickles the surface of the water-carved rocks ...ng Blue Rock Creek in the Sheep River Valley, Kananaskis ...untry.

above:
Steep hillsides and mixed aspen and spruce forests
characterize the area around the Sheep River, Kananaskis
Country.

opposite:
The cabins of Lake O' Hara Lodge, nestled quaintly in Yoho
National Park, provide a deluxe backcountry experience in
a spectacular setting.

above:
Turn off Lake Minnewanka Road to enjoy a quiet picnic at
Cascade Ponds, in Banff National Park. The grassy, wide-open
meadow is a perfect spot to toss around a Frisbee or play
badminton.

opposite:
The Banff Springs Hotel is perched high above the
rushing white waters of Bow Falls. It is one of the most
photographed hotels in Canada.

osite:
...uth of Highwood Pass, along Highway 40, there is the
...e-visited Cat Creek Falls. This beautiful Kananaskis
...untry canyon is home to the falls as well as a variety
...colourful rocks that speckle the stream.

ve:
... recreation area at Paine Lake, near Mountain View
...outhern Alberta, provides an ideal foreground for
... reflections of the distant peaks of Waterton Lakes
...ional Park.

above:
This photograph, taken in Waterton Lakes National Park in
Alberta, reveals an unusually placid Upper Waterton Lake.
Normally, the lake shimmers in sparkling waves from the
nearly constant wind that whips through the valley.

opposite:
Sunset Pass in Banff National Park offers incredible views of
Mount Wilson lit by the setting sun.

pages 62–63:
The dock in the Third Vermilion Lake, in Banff National
Park, offers a contemplative view of Mount Rundle in the
afterglow of a sunset.

ABOUT THE PHOTOGRAPHER

Darwin Wiggett is one of Canada's top landscape photographers and has numerous books to his credit including *Dances With Light — The Canadian Rockies, How to Photograph the Canadian Rockies, Niagara Falls, Amazing Photos — Alberta Landscapes, Amazing Photos — Niagara Falls,* and *Amazing Photos — Prairie Provinces.* He also teaches photography workshops and courses. For more information or to contact Darwin, you can visit www.darwinwiggett.com.

PHOTO CREDITS

All photos are copyright of Darwin Wiggett/Natural Moments Photography. Darwin would like to acknowledge Peter Jeune of The Camera Store in Calgary (www.thecamerastore.com) and Bob Singh of Singh-Ray Filters (www.singh-ray.com) for continued long-term support of his photographic endeavours. Gracious thanks also extend to Reg and Clara Wiggett, April Hamilton, Anita Dammer, and Samantha Chrysanthou for their love and support. Thanks also to Samantha Chrysanthou for her help editing early drafts of this book.